Angelo Tondini Quarenghi

BETWIXT NATURE AND PASSION

Montalcino and Gianfranco Soldera's Brunello

SOLDERA

Veronelli Editore

Editor's note

In a letter to Luigi Veronelli dated 15th December 1989, Gianfranco Soldera wrote: "… these experiences of mine (of the 1989 vintage I have harvested only 30% of the Intistieti grapes) convince me more and more that only with a great grape can you make a great wine; the most you can obtain in the wine cellar is to do as little damage as possible to the quality of the grapes".

I've read this passage I don't know how many times: it sums up Soldera's thought as a whole, more than anything I can say, and it underlines perhaps the greatest merit both of the man and the vine dresser: that stentorian effort – veiled beneath the sweet chubbiness of his figure- of invariably making "extreme" choices, as much in his work as in his life, even when it goes against his interests.

This statement is not in itself original: it becomes so, and takes on immense significance, due to the extent and the sincerity with which Gianfranco has put (and puts) these words into action.
Not only regarding the issue of quality, though this has its importance, but rather for the way –I would say almost in osmosis- that he sees the relationship with the land: love her, respect her, listen to her, reprimand her, thank her (even when she isn't generous); she will repay you in equal measure what you give to her.

It is actually from the intensity of this man-nature relationship that the idea of the book was born: it puts down in writing and celebrates at the same time, a simple yet forcible story. Narrated through the words, both in prose and in poetry, and through the - almost "immaculate", Pascoli-style - images of Angelo Tondini Quarenghi.

This publication is Gianfranco's homage to himself and also his way of repaying everyone - his family first and foremost (I'm thinking in particular of his wife Graziella and her amazing garden, in the words of Hermann Hesse: "Gardening has something similar to the pleasure of creation: you can mould a piece of land into a sea of colour…") – all those who day by day have helped him build Case Basse, namely his farming dream.

Gian Arturo Rota

Nunc vino pellite curas
Now chase your cares away with wine.

Horatio, Odes 1,7,31

Et vinum laetificiet cor hominis!
Let wine lighten the hearts of men!

Psalms, 103,15

Summary

Background History

Background History

Gianfranco Soldera was born in Treviso in 1937. In 1972 he bought the Case Basse farm in Montalcino (Siena). The property covers 24 hectares of which 7 are woodland.

And they say heredity has nothing to do with it!
His grandfather, Luigi, made Raboso wine
near Treviso; his father, Eugenio, loved a drop
of the good stuff, he was a real expert on wine,
his mother was an excellent cook: home, after all,
is where you start educating the taste buds.
The Solderas lost their land: they were against the Fascist regime.
His great-grandparents on his mother's side
lived in San Biagio di Collalta,
and they were wine-makers, too.
His cousins still live there and make good quality wine.
Wine is this family's heart and soul.
Born in Treviso, Gianfranco was three months old when they moved
to Milan. There he grew up, studied and worked for years.
But that secret love for wine never disappeared.
He looked for land all over Piedmont, the Venice area, Tuscany,
and, after years of patient searching, came a gift from the hands of fate:
an abandoned farm in Montalcino in the heart of the Brunello grape lands,
just a handful of derelict houses, considered unsuitable for vines.
It was love at first sight with hard cash being invested
and time, weekends and holidays, always there working.
Then at last farewell to Milan, to live for ever on his farm,
two strong arms taken from business in the north
and restored to the land in Italy's rural womb.
Tuscany, land of beauty and genteel generosity.
But the local producers, the folk from round about,
have never taken to this northerner
who created superlative wines in next to no time
and doesn't play by the rules of advertising and exchange
those gifts and public relations, geared
towards the specialist press.

If...

If...

Making good wine is not easy.
Making great wine is an art.
It takes inspiration, passion,
moderation, sense of smell and culture;
it takes the ability to make decisions and to change;
it takes good quality land that catches the sun just right,
the purest light and air, sunshine, an unspoilt environment;
natural fertilizers, irreprehensible pruning,
careful selection of the grape bunches;
it takes being able to look to the future,
alongside able, tireless assistants;
you have to bet on quality,
you have to invest and not save money,
you mustn't look for easy gains:
it takes good taste and aesthetic sensitivity.
It takes a good measure of wisdom
and a great love for the land;
you have to be willing to work all year round,
in all the seasons and at any time of the day or night:
you have to devote yourself to your vineyard
as to a son or daughter, a child you bring up
whatever the season...
If you can count on all of this
then you have a one
in a hundred chance
of making a great wine.

Habitat

Habitat

In life's cycle that teems around
the green lung of the rows of vines,
the woodland-garden-pond system
creates a balance in the environment.
Graziella yearned for it in her own style
and has moulded and built it up year after year
through tireless dedication,
not with the presumption of being a creator,
but with the patience of one who makes
an already lovely piece of jewellery even more valuable
by embellishing it, by inlaying
and setting precious stones and pearls.
The warm pond-water cradles
thousands of different insects,
nourishment for the great tits and the bats
that find nesting boxes prepared for them here.
And the frogs and the toads, the grass snakes and the vipers:
each species keeps a check on the other,
keeping the numbers down and creating the right balance.
It's a perfect circle of life;
it includes wild boars,
porcupines, foxes, weasels and martens,
bees, wasps and all the pollinating insects.
A miniature cosmos taken back a few centuries
to before weed-killers and fertilizers with devastating chemicals,
before industry and pollution changed
the face of the blue planet.
And the woodland, seven hectares of it, a small Amazon forest
of oaks and junipers, ilexes and laurels,
dogwoods, strawberry trees and elders…
The green lung that makes the air breathable
for you, for us, for the earth and the vines,
it's the barrier that blocks the nasty winds

and it's home to the animals.

Case Basse is a real Time Machine,
a leap backwards to go forwards:
here, pared back to its original state, there's
the soil, the countryside, the surrounding scenery.
Twice a year Sergio Abram, their expert,
checks on the artificial nesting boxes,
put up for birds, bats and insects.
His report is music to the ears
of Nature-lovers:
an inventory that includes hornets, bumble bees,
wasps, dormice, spiders, lizards and starlings,
great tits, tree sparrows,
Liesler noctules, Venus' flying traps…
235 little sleeping places are already there (but there'll be more!),
welcoming havens for all the species.
A great wine requires a habitat
that is complete, unspoilt, in a word – perfect.

Case Basse is a mine of study and experiment. Large sums of money are invested every year under the supervision of expert advisers. 12 university theses at various university faculties, have already been written using Case Basse as their subject material. Professor Attilio Scienza from Milan University holds lectures here and sends his students to gather information.

Professor Sergio Abram, a famous environmental specialist, comes to Case Basse once a year to check on the state of the food chain and the diverse species present in the area. He checks therefore on the hundreds of artificial nesting boxes which have been put up all over the farm to encourage and help insects, birds and chiropters make their homes here.

In 1994, Soldera stipulated a research agreement with the University of Florence under the guidance of Professor Massimo Vincenzini, Head of the Microbiology Department, which allows regular, systematic chemical and microbiological analyses to be carried out from the maturing of the grapes through to the bottling of the wine.

Also Professor Giuseppe Surico, a plant pathologist who studies the terrible vine disease known as "mal dell'esca" also collaborates with Case Basse.

A research project which will last several years has been set up centred on the problems concerning water stress on the vines alongside the Catholic University of Piacenza under the direction of Professor Mario Fregoni, an illustrious expert authority on wine-growing and famous all over the world for his studies. The data gathered from these study projects and the results obtained, contribute to creating a specific heritage which is to the forefront and unique in the world for the scientific community. At the same time, all the research and experimentation carried out allow Case Basse to get a deeper knowledge of the marvels of the world of Nature offering the chance to improve the environment and thus to obtain huge benefits for Soldera's wines.

I have had a double privilege; the chance of going to Case Basse and the fortune of having become a friend of the owners. The third privilege presents itself now – the chance to talk about it.

Going to Case Basse is always a pleasure, a discovery, a surprise. Passing through Montalcino and following the road as it bends and curves towards my destination is a joy in itself. The landscape is among the most beautiful Tuscany has to offer, but it gives you no idea of what lies in store behind the gates of the winery, home to Gianfranco and Graziella Soldera, the two eclectic, friendly and, why not, genial owners of Case Basse.

My relationship with Gianfranco began on a working basis over eleven years ago. His love and passion for wine and his pride in the produce from his vineyards prompted him to study the micro-organisms which transform his grapes into something unique of extraordinary fragrance and flavour. Since then his curiosity as a producer has nurtured and increased my own from a study viewpoint. And the relationship which has grown between us has become a harmonious affinity of passion, experience and science. Beside an extraordinary man you find an exceptional woman. Graziella has worked a miracle. At Case Basse she has created one of the most enchanting private gardens, struggling against the harshness of the terrain, certainly not the easiest to use for such a purpose. But after her expertly passionate care, the original landscape has changed to look gradually like a botanical oasis with an infinite variety of plants and flowers of every shade and colour. Passing through the gates of Case Basse has therefore this double impact: the vineyard and the garden. You can find Gianfranco in the vineyard at any time of the year. He is the one in fact who oversees all the winemaking activities, from the winter pruning to the thinning out of the bunches in summer, from harvesting to the choosing of the grapes. And again in the cellars it is he who follows every step of the transformation of his grapes into wine and the slow maturing of his wine in the big wooden casks.

Instead, in the garden the undisputed sovereign is Graziella. She is always there, active and untiring, the absolute protagonist of every choice in everything that needs done.

The path winds from the old group of farm buildings to the place which celebrates the magic of the wine, the poetry of the garden and the intimacy of the family all at once. It is the new wine cellar and also the new Soldera residence.

The wine cellar was Gianfranco's baby and is the result of a technique in complete respect of Nature. It contains both engineering innovations and love of tradition. The large oak casks carry out their task in an environment which has the feel of an ancient Romanesque cathedral where steel plinths take the place of stone columns.

Above the wine cellar, the house is admirable in the way it blends into the landscape. But it is also amazing how much you feel you are at one with the environment inside the house, too, so much so that there is a continuity with the vineyard and the garden which reaches to its doors. Actually, it comes right up to the house, thanks to the large flower boxes Graziella has laid outside the front door. I could go on for ages talking about Case Basse and its inhabitants but every tale, however detailed, could never bring across to you the enchantment and the emotions that one feels actually living there, relishing its precious wine in the company of Graziella and Gianfranco.

With immense gratitude,

Massimo Vincenzini
Head of the Microbiology Department
Florence University

A TASTE OF SOLDERA

The title here is ambivalent. It refers both to the Brunello di Montalcino wine and to the man himself.

I met him be chance, many years ago, in a petrol station on the motorway. Then we lost sight of each other for years. Then recently my friend Professor Giancarlo Spezia took me to Case Basse because Soldera's Brunello is more worthy of note that a great Burgundy. And the character himself is full of initiatives and new creations. Like the good Milanese chap he is, he never sits around doing nothing and he has a heart of gold.

After studying the Barolo wine and the area it comes from, Soldera gave up his business in Milan and chose another philosophy of life at Case Basse to have his dream of making a great wine come true. He came here because he made the correct assessment of the Case Basse *terroir,* the factor he puts at the top of his list in hiswine-making strategy choices which aim for high quality. Even today he still maintains that you cannot make a great Brunello if the soil and the climate do not also bend towards excellence. He has planted only the sangiovese grape because he respects the discipline which sees it exclusively in purity. He has applied winemaking techniques which respect the environment along with the inflexible picking out of the best bunches during the green harvest (thinning out) followed by the selection of the bunches to use as they come into the cellars before they are pressed. Then come long pulping and ageing processes with a total absence of *barriques* but with prolonged refining in the reducing stage, that is, in the bottle. This is how the Institieti was born, in poor soil, rich framework, vine roots reaching deep into the ground and benefiting from steady, moderate watering. We have drunk it with plain and choice dishes and even with fish: excellent. Soldera's Brunello does not cover the flavours of dishes because its tannins are sweet, but it does not allow itself to be covered by other flavours. It is elegant with a very mineral flavour, persistent scent and the typical soft colour of the sangiovese, never brilliant or intense.

It is worthwhile going to visit Soldera, not just for the vineyards and his modern wine cellar, but also for the warmth and hospitality of his home. Not forgetting the beauty of the large garden abounding in many varieties of roses and other ornamental plants and also fruit trees. This is Signora Graziella's kingdom, where she gathers the whole family round the table at mealtimes, her own offspring and her lovely grandchildren. Case Basse is heaven on earth.

And Gianfranco is the patriarch. You have to recognize this in order to understand this man's personality, his love for the land and for wine. He is open-minded towards innovations but always with respect towards tradition. He is alive to research initiatives (at his expense he hosts surveys on the resistance of the Sangiovese to stress) and to those concerning the development and promotion of the Brunello di Montalcino which he considers the most representative and well-known Italian wine on the market abroad. He rightly maintains that he has to show an example.

The man, his land and his wine. A trilogy which Soldera has blended into an original cru different from all the others because it reflects the character and the passion of both the producer and the *terroir.*

Mario Fregoni
Professor of Viticulture
Catholic Sacro Cuore University – Piacenza
OIV Honorary President
President of the International Academy of Sensory Analysis

I met Franco over thirty years ago and since then the faith he has placed in me has equalled my friendship. In all these years of deep and shared esteem, I believe I have worked with him towards creating many very great wines.

Giulio Gambelli

The Soldera bottle label was designed by Piero Leddi.

Wine

Wine

It's like a work of art: technique is of secondary importance.
Culture and a keen sense of smell are what's needed,
good quality land,
an unmarred environment pared down to its original state.
You need to love what you do;
wine is not just one product
but many things put together.
If even just one of these things is missing
a balance is broken, it spoils everything,
the whole thing comes down like a castle made of playing cards.

Striving for quality: that's the point.
There was a time when great care was taken in the search
for beauty and excellence. Then the masses
came to prefer the façade to what lies behind it.
Today the label is more important than the wine. Madness.
A great wine is for the few, because it costs effort and money.
But when the job is done well, there's no need for advertising.
It's *quality* that sells.

34

The Third Millennium

The Third Millennium

Man's present dimension
stems from intuition and research
thanks to our fellow men
from Archimedes to Einstein
from Socrates to Voltaire and Popper.
Theories, solutions, discoveries
to open our minds
to make life easier, to help struggle
against Mother Nature who is lovely to look at
but often is less mother and more step-mother.
"But she's never a stepmother", says Franco,
"we're the ones who treat her badly: she just keeps us at bay.
She is only violent if we are".

We now control matter using physics
we control life genetically.
The question we must now ask ourselves is:
would we be worse off without atomic energy
without bio-technology? Perhaps not.
But would we be better off without Soldera's wine?
Most assuredly not, of that we can be certain.
"He who has not tasted cannot understand".

The Vineyard

The Vineyard

When you came to Case Basse, Franco,

there were no vines: it's unbelievable.

The land was untilled and empty!

Now the vineyard is your laboratory

and it keeps you occupied every day of the year,

like a very beautiful

but very, very demanding lover.

Everything is done by hand here: topping,

tying back, thinning out and pruning.

A couple of buds on each spur:

you place your bet on a single bunch.

You pick off the grapes damaged in the hailstorms

one by one,

you prune by the light

of the waning moon,

you work the soil with care,

you scatter the oat straw that allows the soil

to breathe and protects the roots;

you strengthen the vines with propolis.

Then you proudly show off

your store of cow dung from the Val di Chiana,

that softens and enriches the soil.

"Lots of folks use chemical fertilizers,

weed-killers and systemics,"

you say, shaking your head, "and then it all

ends up in the wine. Idiots!"

The New Wine Cellar

The New Wine Cellar

It was certainly not chance but necessity
that prompted you to build the new cellar.
The old one was small, with hardly room to swing a cat,
it was split into two and awkward
and in summer it was so hot that every day
you had to keep cooling off the floor.
It was too much for a perfectionist like you,
tormented as you are by a passion for excellence.
A great hole in the ground
then steel pylons, the floor and the walls,
built with tons of gravel,
just stones wedged into wire netting,
with no cement cast, no plaster,
none of the technology that is homologating the planet.

"The cobbled floor has to breathe,
the ceiling has to breathe, the whole building
has to be able to breathe, just like an animate being",
you say, as if you were talking about a child.
The huge grotto that will cherish your wine,
that will let it age more slowly than before,
at a constant temperature, the air circulating
naturally inside, like a chimney that doesn't smoke.
You have said your Brunello
will be fifty per cent better for it!
Impossible, Franco, that's impossible.
You have always been close to perfection,
one mark off it, a mere nothing, and you know it.

CASE BASSE: NATURE, DIMENSION, HARMONY
by the architect Stefano Lambardi

As you come near the "Piagge di Maremma" you look over towards the horizon, across the hills which mark the boundary of the Ombrone valley.

The countryside is sweetly rolling and decorated by human hand in the patterns of the ploughed fields. It is one side of the hill at Montalcino, the one that faces west which the sun always shines on, almost as if he were highlighting his power over the land.

The hill-slope as you descend is criss-crossed by little lanes which form a network, a mesh in which the farms become single stitches of this land-system. As you travel towards this area of Montalcino you are surrounded by "landscape", soaked in dimensions and ratios of scale that chop and change all the time: long rows of trees, woods, ploughed fields and vineyards bring first one object, or rather subject, to the fore in this or that image. Perhaps travellers who described our nation at the end of last century were talking about just these sensations, showing how important all these elements are within the landscape. Each is part of a picture in scale and makes up a landscape; in this way a close up is created, or else a background.

The Case Basse project came from the deep relationship man has with the landscape. Born of the respect that comes from the feeling that you are *inside* nature, part and parcel of a whole that defines each step you take, that guides you in the power of reasoning that our culture has. Or rather, that our being Nature's respectful and dedicated sons and daughters has.

Gianfranco Soldera has grasped the meaning of this deep relationship that we have always had with Nature in his work, in his wine-making: that *mimesis* which is imitation and exchange. Man's encounter with Nature is, and perhaps will always be, the real theme on which to base a discussion of why we are here; the relationship with the land and the laws that govern it, while trying to get from it the best that it can give, in full respect of those laws, has always driven us. This is what Soldera has placed his bets on. In every conversation you have with Soldera these beliefs and firm convictions transpire. With him they become almost intransigence, a trait at times necessary in a man who knows the challenge he has undertaken.

Nature is *"in charge"* at Case Basse, and there is no way that technology can take over her role. Being able to recognize this, in the age of technological advance, and relish this totally nihilistic analytical-cum-technical-cum-scientific thought is an act of great courage and also great respect – then again, gifts needed in any commander.

So this project comes from Nature and from Her elements, water, (the source of primordial life) stone (from Gaia, from Mother Earth's womb) and from the relationship these elements have with the natural agents of heat and cold. It comes from the desire for self-protection, or rather to protect the fruits of man's toil, almost a return to the womb, a chance to incubate and ensure that everything happens at just the right moment.

In order to build the wine cellar we dug down several metres to try and create a sort of grotto using only natural materials, stone and iron, without any contribution from chemistry which changes the cards on the table and produces extraordinary, but uncontrollable, effects. And just like in a grotto, we let the air circulate freely so that the protective and not dissolute side to matter could come from the depths of the earth. The ground, the earth, is conceived as a positive element, a prelude to the issuing forth of the event, not as something negative and destructive.

The Case Basse wine cellar was born of that "dimension of the land" and the relationship with where it lies; the actual buildings are at either end which, through its shape, was the attempt to render the end of a journey. A simple wall and square copper roof covering stands in the middle to underline the top of the "head", where everything ends and you have to retrace your steps.

Case Basse is "dimension" and "reason", in the classical meaning of the term. It is the dimension which allows us to come to know Nature, to be able to understand Her and copy Her perfection. It is the reasoning which guides our thoughts and always has, and which allows us to overcome our fear of "kaos". But more than anything else, we like to think that everything has been planned with an eye to total harmony.

The drawings of the views of the new wine cellar are by the artist Piero Leddi.

Piero Leddi   Montalcino   8 Genn. 2001

Piero Leddi   Montalcino   8 Genn. 2001

The Garden

The Garden

for Graziella

A couple of hectares of garden are not

just flowers, colours and things of beauty,

they also extend the cycle of life

that is a by-word by now for the Solderas.

You flit back and forth in this enchanted,

joyful place like a good fairy:

watering and pruning,

planting and weeding,

hard-working as a conscientious

labourer, as a mother toiling

to raise the creatures she loves.

There are fifteen hundred rose varieties

(some refined for years

and found only in far off places

like Texas or Australia);

your collection of American irises,

purple, gold and black (so much loved by the porcupines!)

and the beautiful Lilium Soldera, ruby red in colour,

created by Fletter, producer of hybrids

in honour of your Brunello.

You yearned for the *white garden* to attract

the night-time pollinators,

to transmit life even in the silent darkness.

Graziella, there stand your beloved Chinese apple trees,

small and seemingly useless

since their fruits get thrown away.

Yet, in April, the blossoms are irresistible

in their oriental airiness,

their elegance indispensable

to the beauty of their environment,

one hundred and four miracles

of different species and colours.

Your work is therefore fundamental,
such an important piece of the mosaic.
And a joy to the eyes.

A great wine is created in the garden as well.
The knack is to match
the flowering times,
not forcing them,
not looking for special effects,
composing, gathering together, supervising,
harmonizing colours, shapes and *nuances*.

Portrait

Portrait

In his vineyards and wine cellars, Gianfranco
becomes an amiable tyrant
in blue overalls and gumboots.
There's no questioning his orders:
they are just to be carried out. He's a dangerous man to contradict.
"It's true", he admits, "I'm a centralizer,
I expect people to do things the way I want them done:
it's the result that counts.
But I do listen to advice from others,
I accept criticism and thank you for it.
I have no technological learning,
but my own vision of the world
and I put it into practice in my vineyard, too."

All the same, in the end, Soldera the indomitable,
becomes a skilful sorcerer
and from an abandoned farm
he has been able to conjure up the nectar
that makes life sweet.
Not tyrant, then, but *princeps*.
To the man who defines himself " a model of presumption"
we make a toast: "Let presumption always be with you!"

The Family

The Family

A woman who would follow you
in your gamble of a lifetime
wasn't all that easy to find.
And yet, like for wine, you had
a good nose for her, too: Graziella is
a really first-rate companion,
perhaps the only one who takes you as you are.
Your kids have beaten other tracks
but are slowly making their way back to you,
just as you have always wanted and hoped they would.
Mauro (skilful, with a perfect sense of timing,
he goes straight to the heart of any problem
and he's got a keen sense of smell, too), will descend
upon Case Basse one of these days with his Beba in tow
to make great wine, maybe
different from yours: that's fine by you.
Monica has already chosen the country.
Away from Milan with her beloved Paolo,
Costanza, Arianna and the twins, Mathilde and Emma,
she delights in the pure air of Tuscany.
She is a top class manager and she'll see
to your beloved Brunello. Beloved by one and all.
You were right in that, too, leaving your kids free
to try other things and put themselves to the test.
Now you wait for them to come sailing
like ships into port after a long time at sea.
Case Basse is – and will remain – in good hands.

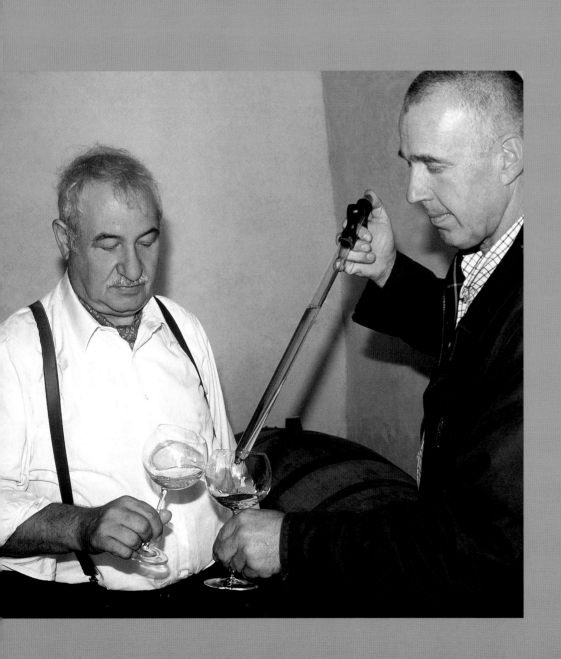

The Friends

The Friends

Angelo, whose eyes have seen the beauty
of Nature all over the world;
Piero, the artist, who with the thrills he can give
is a source of constant surprise;
Sandro, Armando, Agostino,
Ezio, Marco Prete and Paolo Lucchesi
always ready and willing;
Mauro, the hideaway, but a precious friend;
Rino, the researcher of gastronomic delights;
Piero, nicknamed the *"muset"*;
Stefano, the architect, whose desire is
that Soldera's wine were less well-known,
"the more word gets out, the less there is for us to drink!"
he says selfishly simplistic about it.
Riccardo, from Prato, has a witty tongue
and keeps everyone amused;
Federico, the lawyer,
Stefano, the grand gentleman from Prato;
Sergio, the environmentalist,
Fabio, whose corks are the best in the world;
Graziano, Valeriano, Fabiano, Massimo, Luca, Emanuele
Cesare and Pietro, all able salesmen;
Peligio, Peppino, Orlando and Giampiero,
Enrico "the cook", Carlo,
Federico and Alberto, Sally.

Giulio, whose nose is the most sensitive in the world;
Beppe, the fragrance of truffles in the Barolo;
Marco, who illustrates the marvels of Sicily's wines;
Pino, nights spent in the cellar tasting and chewing the fat,
Walter, whose love for his native Irpinia oozes from every pore.

With Gravner Gianfranco's understanding
has deeply paternal and brotherly undertones.
Josko produces the best Italian white wine,
a divine Ribolla, in his cellars in Oslavia.
Gianfranco holds him in high esteem
but gives him lots of new advice,
pushing him towards perfection,
just as he does himself, every day.
This, his one true curse:
a strong passion for excellence.

Then there is Attilio, the walking encyclopaedia of grape vines;
Massimo, the illustrious microbiologist
who widens and deepens
his knowledge all the time.
Marco Fregoni, the hugely knowledgeable professor;
Giancarlo Spezia and Andrea Paoletti;
Valerio, the expert agronomist; Salvatore Maule.
Franco Biondi Santi, ever ready to fight
for Montalcino and the Brunello wine.
Giulio Gambelli, a friend and almost a brother
for thirty years, who alongside Franco
has created the greatest of wines.

And the fond memory of Luciano, the friend from way back;
of Giovanni, the *"Monfortino"*
an exceptionally unassuming person
and an unbridgeable void in the world of wine;
of Edgardo "a shining light of civility for the world";
of Gino Veronelli, the poet, who fought and did so much for wine;
of Bartolo Mascarello, the conscience of the Langhe region;
of Floriano Bodini, the sculptor;
of Arnaldo and Ginetta, of Nando.

Beyond the Garden

After the generous glasses of wine at lunch
we rested beside the column
in that peerless garden of yours.
Mexican clouds as the backdrop,
clouds of cumulus-nimbus, luminous and still,
light fluffy clusters of creamy white cirrus,
total silence broken only now and again
by the roar of a jet, high up in the sky,
or by the constant metallic clunk
of a Chinese mechanical bird
stirred by the light breeze.
For once there were no insects to bother us:
Flies, ants, wasps
and busy bumble bees kept away.
Nothing and nobody disturbed our total
abandon, the general rehearsal
for perfect peace, for that final journey.

Beyond the Garden

Summer at Case Basse

The large sangiovese,
these small August grapes
coming on well, nearly ready
for the next grape harvest
are the mastery of probability
the exultation of diversity,
in the sour taste of their juice,
each one varying from its neighbour,
in the same bunch, from the same vine.
A miracle.
Meanwhile, in the new cellars,
they're bringing out old vats and brand new casks.

Summer at
Case Basse

Gems of wisdom from Gianfranco

My search for harmony

Tradition is often stupid because men tend to follow in each other's mistakes. Each generation copies the one before and loses rationality and wisdom.

In order to have progress someone has to throw away his riches. If share cropping hadn't ended, I wouldn't be here.

Today, as in the past, the really good things are only for the few because there isn't enough for everyone. If you produce more, the quality deteriorates.

The small artisan cannot really compete against the large companies. But when you compare the goods produced, it gets embarrassing because of the difference in quality. So the company tries to eliminate the artisan by offering much lower prices.

Wine is made in the vineyards not in the wine cellar.

There are no more than 50 really great wines in the world because the great winegrowing lands are so few.

Everything comes together in Nature; it's there you find an explanation for everything, from life through to death.

The first thing I look for in my wine cellar is harmony.

The land always needs looking after, it needs daily care. A factory needs much less.

As far as wine is concerned, Italy is unparalleled in the world. But we don't know how to make the most of it.

I could make 60 thousand bottles a year instead of my usual 15 thousand. But I put my money on absolute quality. Wine is like a diamond: if it's cut badly you lose all its value.

I make wine above all because I like drinking it. It's an excellent product, it's genuine, it's almost a medicinal cure.

To make a good wine you need a good nose. Smell is the first of the senses used in taste, it's the most important.

The quality of the soil, plus the habitat, plus the winemaker's ability together make a great wine. But if even only one of these 3 things is not at its utmost, then the whole thing collapses.

Never make a promise you can't keep: otherwise you'll end up a slave.

Beauty and goodness take a lot out of you.

Ignorance is often countrified because what is lacking is comparison and a chance to experiment.

School from the age of three to ten should only revolve around: drama, music, two hours of running every day, walks through the woods and in gardens, visits to museums and cities of art.

Harmony and proportion have to be the basis of every one of man's actions.

A great wine

You can tell a great wine by its harmony, elegance, complexity and naturalness.

This means balance and proportion, refinement and manifold sensations of aroma and taste. It means using mature, healthy grapes, transformed naturally into alcohol, following their natural process, with no chemical products or colouring added.

A great wine gives satisfaction, a sense of well-being, the desire to drink it again; it creates and increases conviviality and friendship. It is unique, rare, typical and long-lived. In it you can recognize its micro-territory, the vineyard it hails from. The wine from the Instistieti cru for example is different from the wine that comes from the Case Basse vineyard although no distance at all separates them.

A great wine cannot be substituted, because it has unique features, like any work of art. I sold not one bottle of 1989 vintage because I did not consider it up to my usual high standards of quality.

A great wine is rare, the tip of the pyramid of around 20 billion bottles produced around the world every year. No more than 50 or 60 thousand of them will ever reach the top.

A great wine is long-lived: it must improve, at least in the first twenty years, and give different sensations as time passes. It is the only natural food product that has a longer life-span than a man's.

All these features raise the production costs considerably – and the price – of a great wine. But any producto which has similar worth is never going to come cheap. Beauty and excellence take time, experience and large investments.

I produce an average of 15 thousand bottles a year. But I drastically reduce that number if, because of bad weather conditions during the season, the grape harvest is not up to scratch. Out of 30 vintages, 27 have been excellent: a record. The best of the lot, historic, is 1979's..

Wine is however and always will be subjectivity: The same bottle can be worth 500 euros to one person and not even 1 euro to another.

Gianfranco Soldera

Montalcino

or rather of the sublime

Montalcino
or rather of the sublime

For years I've driven down all the roads that lead into Montalcino. I have come down from the north, from Asciano, passing through Buonconvento, or cutting left towards San Giovanni d'Asso. Sometimes I would arrive from the east via Pienza and San Quirico; or maybe from the south via the Val d'Orcia, from Poggio alle Mura; and even from the west via Bagni di Petriolo, passing through Selceta and Poggio La Vigna.

The very names in this area were enough to send that special shiver down my spine: Murlo, Castiglione del Bosco, Torrenieri, Lama. Along these narrow, windy roads, in the heart of scenery virtually unchanged for centuries, I would go back to the deepest Middle Ages.

I've always come to these parts like a layman on pilgrimage, much as the most devout Christians at one time went from Burgundy to Compostela along the Milky Way. Here, mind you, anything that tastes of milk is for children or convalescents. It's a completely different kind of liquid that's drunk here.

I've travelled a lot during my life. My eyes have seen more than half the planet. I might add that I was born in Tuscany, in Arezzo, although I have lived in the north for many years. Now, everyone knows that the inhabitants of Arezzo and Siena don't get on, they never have. But in Tuscany everyone has to have an enemy, otherwise you're not worth a mention, you just don't exist.

And so, if a shrewd, very demanding character from Arezzo can bring himself to admit that this part of the province of Siena has the most beautiful scenery in Italy, in Europe (and consequently in the world), then you can believe it. It's hard for me to admit it, but it's true. I've never seen anything like it on any of my travels. There are incredible concentrations of beauty that are almost menacing. "There is even a greatness which is insulting", Camus used to say and it's so true. Venice is the prime example. I've always taken very bad photographs and written total banalities in Venice. The overdose of beauty I get there gives me writer's cramp.

I go all helpless and all I can do is contemplate. Any additional movement brings only damage and ruin.
The same thing happens to me in Montalcino, in the Val d'Orcia and the Crete area around Siena. I stop in front of a geometrical scene of browns, yellows and greens, an isolated farmhouse, placed there by some great unseen art director and I give up. I look into my camera's viewfinder, I try to zoom in, I hold it upright, horizontal, I try changing lens. Nothing. The result is mediocre, normal, déjà vu. The real thing stands over me and humiliates me. Better to give up.
I've stopped many times in an autumn sunset in Val d'Orcia. Light and dark clods of earth just soaked by the early rains. In the

distance a flock of sheep grazing ever so slowly in the moonlight, almost still. A cypress-tree, the pale moon rising shyly shimmering. What can you do at times like these? Start taking snapshots? Shooting film? Taking notes?
Is it not better just to look, take a deep breath and half-close your eyes to focus on a bush in the foreground and lost way in the background a tiny village with its first lights twinkling? No use documenting, developing films or writing articles, books or poems. It's much better just to give up and drink everything in, recording it in your memory.
I once took three American friends with me in and around Montalcino. They were lost for words they were so enchanted by the wondrous composure of the vineyards and the olive groves facing Sant'Antimo. They gave in straight away to the power that stood over them. It was then I tried introducing the "deception theory".
"Look", I said. "Look carefully. All this wonder is a bluff, nothing but a bluff. This landscape you see unfold before you like one of Topor's paintings is a total fake. You're contemplating the beauties of nature, God Almighty, the Creation, this wonderful land that we have been given. Wrong. What you see before you is of man's making, it's all his work. The Tuscan countryside is artificial, designed and created by simple folk over hundreds and hundreds

of years. Take the cypresses. Not one of them is there by chance. All accurately planted in a particular place. They always point to something: a church, a villa, a graveyard, the boundaries of someone's land, a farmhouse, a "maestà" (one of those small altars dedicated to the Madonna), a crossroads. They are signposts, tall, slim, elegant sentries with a precise meaning decided for, and given to them, by man. The same as the vineyards, the olive groves, the fields of corn and sunflowers, the vegetable gardens and the orchards, the dykes and the houses. A sublime harmony created and devised by man. One of the rare times when our handiwork has not spoilt but rather enhanced the landscape, enriching it with colours, shapes and geometric figures. I know of only one other similar case: the paddy fields of Bali in Indonesia. With the work of centuries there they have cut into the hills, building canals and raising banks for the rice crops. The effect is extraordinary. There are times of the day, especially at sunset, when the narrow fields, cut out from the hillsides and flooded, become a system of mirrors which reflect the sky. It's an optical and pictorial illusion of incredible intensity.

Right, now look around you. Mother nature hasn't been defeated here, she's been interpreted and remodelled by man. After watching and taking note, she would now like to imitate our handiwork, but she can't: it's too difficult."

Soldera, a dear friend of mine for more than twenty years now, lives not far from Montalcino. He is not from Tuscany originally, he's from the north. One day he quit everything, sold up his business and his house. He bought land here, renovated old farm buildings, planted new vines, investing all the money he possessed. I'm sure he must have his problems, just like everyone else. But I know he wouldn't go back for anything in the world.

He lives in a place of such beauty that it could be spoilt by a mere nothing. A tree displaced, a road asphalted, the wrong colour or even a noise, can make the whole picture collapse, like blowing on a castle made of playing cards. From the people around here he has slowly made his that inborn love of perfection that will be his curse for the rest of his days. He has learnt their fascination for restraint, the ability to stop and not overdo things, which is the secret in creating a work of art. In a land like this where the greatest insult is "you always go too far!", it's no joke.

A mistake which deceives or upsets the senses, which changes the

rules of an ancient game, the clauses of a centuries-old pact, is a mistake which will never be forgiven. The folk around here are very friendly, but don't ever go too far because the reaction could well be violent. In the name of what? Gracious! Of aesthetics, beauty and harmony, of course, the continual search for balance between shape and form, between appearances and what lies behind them. Why, what did you think?: money, power, success? Wrong. Here, we're in another dimension.

Here, the countryside not only has to produce, it has to please and fulfil the senses. Did you know that they have genetically "built" a cow in Holland with an enormous udder that produces fantastic quantities of milk? Well, they haven't managed to sell even one of them in Tuscany. The reason: because it's ugly.

Gianfranco has adapted positively to the philosophy of the area, but then again, he had little choice in the matter. He is more Tuscan than I am now. Each time I visit him he gives me some of his wine and I take the precious bottles back on the motorway, always in the fear that I'll have an accident and they'll get broken.

At this moment it's the dead of night in Milan and I'm writing in the total silence. A milky white mist shrouds the landscape making it look like a creation by a surrealist painter just to spite me. But, luckily I have a glass of Gianfranco's Brunello here beside me and I sip it slowly, my eyes half-closed. Sublime.

Photographs, poems, texts, work plan and project
Angelo Tondini Quarenghi

arcangelo2002@yahoo.it
www.angelotondini.com

Graphic design
Alessandro Villa

Translation into English by
Susan Armstrong

Many thanks go to those who contributed in building the new complex:

Stefano Lambardi – TETRACTIS – design engineer
Fabrizio Maset - TESAM

Banca Toscana
INCA
Banca di Roma

Maurizio Boatto
Silvano Bonciani - Biochemie Lab
Stefano Breda
Carlo Cappellari
Fabrizio Cardini
Cesare Casini
Eliodoro Casu
Gianni Confente - FILA
Franco Crosato -GELA
Alessandro Fedrigo
Albano Fornasier - IMEF
Piero Garbellotto
Leonardo Giannetti

Paolo Leggeri
Angelo Lunardelli
Mario Magagnin
Maurizio Maramai
Roberto Meattini
Alberto Moroni - FASSA
Gianni Ottaviani
Fabiano Piccin
Giuseppe Tagliabue
Fabrizio Tognazzi
Bruno Vanini
Massimo Vincenzini
Valerio Zorzi

Printing:
Euroteam, Nuvolera (BS)

The compiling of this volume was completed on 31st July 2006
Printing concluded during the month of October 2006

SOLDERA

Azienda Agricola Case Basse di Gianfranco Soldera

Località Case Basse - 53024 - Montalcino (Siena Italy)
Telefono and fax ++39 0577 848567

gianfranco.soldera@casebasse.it
www.soldera.it